COMMUNITY FIRST

HOW TO BUILD A DIGITAL COMMUNITY
WITH SUSTAINABLE GROWTH AND
EXPONENTIAL SOCIAL IMPACT

SHANNAN MONSON

Book design by Ariel Garcia
Photography by Laura Metzler

Second edition 2023

SBM Partners
3423 Piedmont Rd NE
Suite 383
Atlanta, GA 30305

www.shannanmonson.com
hello@shannnanmonson.com

THIS BOOK IS DEDICATED TO THE DREAMERS.

The one's who are writing when no one is reading, creating when no one is consuming, and putting in the hours when no one is clapping, no one is watching, no one is listening. To the one's who know hard work is the secret,

THIS ONE'S FOR YOU.

WHAT'S
INSIDE

INTRODUCTION

INVITATION

ADOPTION

ADAPTATION

EXPANSION

WHY COMMUNITY COMES FIRST...

The one constant in life (barring a zombie apocalypse) is people. Technology will change, the environment we live in will change, and the way we live, work, and play will, inevitably, change. But through it all, people will remain at the heart of everything. That's why investing in people—and more specifically—investing in building a community of people— is, in my opinion, the most valuable investment you can make.

Communities have one powerful characteristic: their ability to adapt. Maybe you build a community around a product today that doesn't exist a year from now. Because you built a community, not just a marketing channel for one specific product, you can move on to the next product or idea, with a full community of support alongside you. In other words, you're building a business that stands the test of time.

Maybe you're running for office at the local or national level. Your community won't just help you win the vote now, they'll also mobilize to take action on ideas and create change towards your ideals once you're in office. And when the campaign trail is over, when your term is complete, they'll watch your tv show, buy your memoir, the list goes on...

You might even be all of these things—a social media manager, a government candidate, a business owner, a school leader—at different times in your life, and when you build a strong community around your core values, the community you've built will jump start every single one of your new and next identities. In short, you've made a very smart decision to invest in the power of community. Whatever pivots, adaptations, and new journeys you may take, starting with community first builds a solid foundation. My petition to be your greatest fan starts now.

OVERVIEW

After studying thousands of successful online communities, mentoring hundreds of influencers and entrepreneurs, and building multiple online communities, I've noticed core patterns in the most engaged communities.

This book will walk you through a timeline approach to building community. First, you do this, then you do that. You'll find the four phases to community building on the next page.

Here's another way to look at it: your content strategy needs three types of content. Content that helps new people find you, content that helps you connect with people, and content that helps people take action towards accomplishing your mission.

CONTENT STRATEGY

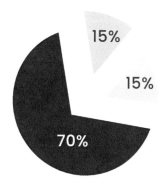

15%

15%

70%

Each community strategy will look different. But on average, a good breakdown of the content you post will look something like this.

Prioritize connection content first, conversion content second, and discovery content once you've proven you can connect with people and convert them to take action.

DISCOVERY

Content that helps new people discover your community

- Shows up on their "For You" page

- Gets re-posted by another account

- Gets promotes through paid ads

- See: Expansion Phase

CONNECTION

Content that adds value and builds connections

- Most of your content

- Invokes emotion

- Builds know, like, and trust

- See: Adoption Phase

CONVERSION

Content that helps people take action towards the mission

- Responds to objections

- Outlines the process

- Shares testimonials or social proof

- Creates urgency to take action

FOUR PHASES OF COMMUNITY

HOW IT WORKS

Based on my experience, there are four major phases of building a successful, engaged community. In this workbook we'll break down the core components of each phase, alongside exercises to help you implement each one. Whether you're starting from scratch or building an established community, look for ways to go deeper, take a different perspective, and add new strategies to your community growth plan.

ADAPTATION

ADOPTION

INVITATION

GROWTH

TIME

EXPANSION

The Art & Science of
Viral Posts
Psychology of Sharing
Capturing Attention

Adapting with Analytics
Responding with Content
A/B Testing for Growth
Leveraging UGC

Content Categories Overview
Content Formats
Content Templaes
Starting Conversations
Creating Experiences

Writing a Mission Statement
Defining Community Values
Creating a Visual Identity
Writing a Bio

 Note:

Your community
should start deep
and go wide over
time. Don't be
afraid to start niche
communities.

PLATFORM COMPARISON

Each social platform has different strengths and weaknesses. The concepts we cover in this workbook are, generally speaking, universal concepts that apply to any social platform because these strategies are based off human behavior, not algorithms.

However, each platform has it's own unique strengths, limitations, and idiosyncracies. This guide is not meant to be a social media growth guide, but rather a guide to building communities on any social media platform.

	PRIORITIZES	BEST FOR YOU IF...
Instagram	photo + short video	aesthetic approach, enjoy creating short-form video + photography
Facebook	text, photo + short video	wide approach of content styles, building groups or long-format
TikTok	short viral videos	fun and relaxed approach, enjoy creating short-form, trend-focused
Twitter	short text snippets	humor or news-centered approach, enjoy writing short-
LinkedIn	long text + blog format	professional approach, enjoy creating work-related content
YouTube	long-format video + shorts	highly creative approach, enjoy creating long-format video

PHASE ONE

INVITATION

01 INVITATION

02 ADOPTION

03 ADAPTATION

04 EXPANSION

WRITING A
MISSION
STATEMENT

PEOPLE DON'T FOLLOW PEOPLE, THEY FOLLOW IDEALS

The first step to building a strong, engaged community is finding a mission people can rally around. Your mission statement isn't just a sentence on a website (that no one reads), it's the common thread that brings people together in the first place.

Think of the communities you are already a part of. They likely all exist because you have a common mission. Church communities exist to bring people closer to their spiritual beliefs. School communities exist to educate students to help build a better world.

Every single community you are a part of has a strong, central mission that connects you—not just to the leader, but to each other.

Your first job, as a community builder, is to define that mission. A great place to start is to follow what really pisses you off, what's broken, and what desperately needs to be fixed. Once you determine that, you can create a mission to change it.

EXAMPLE ONE

When I was given the task of building a community of mothers for a new media company many years ago, the first thing we asked was, what's wrong with the motherhood communities we're already a part of?

The answer was simple. At the time, they were extremely divisive. Working mothers versus stay-at-home mothers, breastfeeding versus bottle feeding, moms were pitted against each other, and we wanted to change that.

So we set out on a mission to redefine motherhood. No matter how you chose to be a mom, we were behind you 100%. The result? A community of tens of thousands of mothers in just a few short months.

EXAMPLE TWO

A few years ago I was approached by an entrepreneur who wanted to build a community empowering women in business.

The first thing I asked was, "Well, there's a lot of communities for women in business. Why should people join this one?" I started asking questions (the same questions I want you to answer on the next page) until we got to a statistic that really upset them. Less than 2% of female-owned businesses ever broke $1 million dollars in revenue. Suddenly, they had a simple, but powerful mission: change the statistics.

When you have a mission people believe in, an ideal that incites action, real community is born. Rather than try to get people to follow you or your brand online, invite people to join you in taking action towards a mission.

EXAMPLES TO JUMPSTART IDEAS

KIDS AND PARENTING

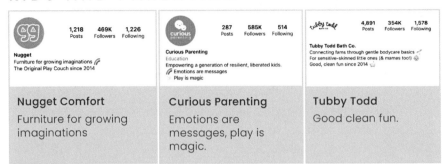

Nugget Comfort

Furniture for growing imaginations

Curious Parenting

Emotions are messages, play is magic.

Tubby Todd

Good clean fun.

LIFESTYLE

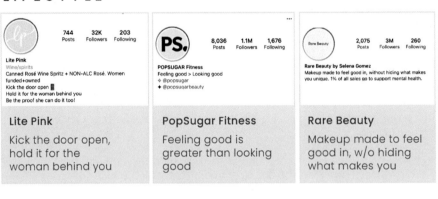

Lite Pink

Kick the door open, hold it for the woman behind you

PopSugar Fitness

Feeling good is greater than looking good

Rare Beauty

Makeup made to feel good in, w/o hiding what makes you

NEWS AND PUBLISHING

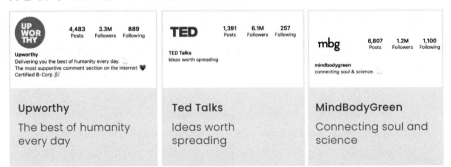

Upworthy

The best of humanity every day

Ted Talks

Ideas worth spreading

MindBodyGreen

Connecting soul and science

MISTAKES TO AVOID

The biggest mistake I see people and brands make when building an online community is putting their own personal goals first. Whether it's selling a product or looking cool because you have followers next to your name, and I can't stress this enough, no one cares about you. They care about what you can do for them. Start with a mission that serves them and you've built the foundation for a real community.

BRAINSTORMING SESSION

What upsets you about your niche or industry?_____

_____

_____

_____

What's broken? What could be better?_____

_____

_____

What topic gets you really excited? _____

_____

_____

_____

What's the ideal result? In a perfect world, what changes?

_____

_____

_____

_____

IN 7 TO 10 WORDS, WRITE A MISSION STATEMENT.

CONGRATS!

You just built the foundation for people to rally around. Give yourself permission to allow this version one to grow, adapt, and change as you learn more about your community. Remember, it doesn't have to be perfect, you just have to start. Give yourself a high five and take a selfie of the moment, one day you'll look back and say this is where it all started. (Brownie points: tag me on social media so I can give you a virtual high five, too.)

DEFINING

COMMUNITY VALUES

HELP THE RIGHT PEOPLE FIND YOU

Your core community values, what you stand for or against, will either attract or repel people from your community. And that's exactly what you want. The strongest communities have common core values and worldviews. By weaving your core values into everything you do (especially into shareable viral quotes) you'll start to help the *right* people discover you.

Start by discerning what your core values are, the list below will help you get started. What values do you want the people in this community to share? What's important to you? Why? Using the exercise on the next page as a starting point, underline all the values that stand out to you. Don't overthink it, just start underlining. Then, narrow it down to 3 core values. Circle them.

You'll lean into your values hard when you start creating content, especially shareable content, which we'll dive deeper into inside the expansion phase of building your community.

CORE COMMUNITY VALUES

Active	Down to Earth	Mature
Adventurous	Dynamic	Minimal
Ambitious	Edgy	Modern
Approachable	Elegant	Natural
Belonging	Fearless	Playful
Bold	Fun	Positive
Brave	Genuine	Professional
Bright	Harmonious	Quirky
Bubbly	Heartfelt	Rest
Calm	Helpful	Relaxed
Candid	High-end	Romantic
Carefree	Honest	Sassy
Casual	Hopeful	Serious
Charming	Inclusive	Sincere
Cheerful	Independent	Sophisticated
Classic	Innovative	Timeless
Collaborative	Inspirational	Traditional
Colorful	Intentional	Transparent
Cool	Inviting	Trendy
Cozy	Joyful	Trustworthy

CHOOSE YOUR VALUES

These will help define your content strategy and drive community growth. You'll lean into these as you create and curate shareable content in the the future.

_____

_____

_____

SHAREABLE VALUE CONTENT

By creating and sharing content specific to your community values, you'll start to attract more of the right people to your community. For example...

IF YOUR VALUES ARE...

REST

what it says: people in our community don't hustle at the expense of their health and relationships. if you share this value, this community is for you.

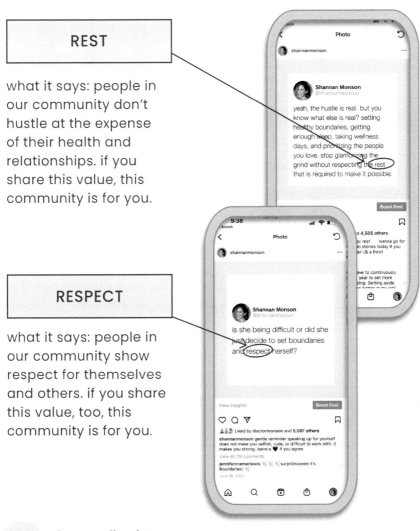

RESPECT

what it says: people in our community show respect for themselves and others. if you share this value, too, this community is for you.

*For a deeper dive into shareable content, see section four: expansion.

VISUAL IDENTITY

THAT STANDS OUT

A strong visual identity is 9 times out of 10, not a luxury but a requirement for building an online community. With so many pages and communities on the internet, unless you are *exceptionally good at something else* (i.e. humor, news, etc) you will most likely want to establish a strong visual presence. This helps to establish your community's credibility, presence as a leader in your space, and immediately tell a story even before someone dives into your content.

Start with the feelings you want your community member to feel, and then work backwards from there. A social media visual identity is typically just an extension of a brand

SIMPLE

With social communities, you'll tell micro stories instead of macro ones. Branded videos, logos, and imagery may work great on your website, you'll probably want to use less branded assets on social media where people see one piece of content at a time. Often, the simplest, least branded content tells the most powerful social stories.

NATIVE

You want your social content to fit within the aesthetic of the platform you're already using. If you're posting to twitter, you'll use text only. If you're posting to Instagram, you'll post video and photos that are native to that platform, etc. When in doubt, less is more. Think about what naturally fits, and adapt your content to feel native to that platform.

TEMPLATIZED

Whether you're starting with a visual identity created by a top tier graphic designer, or starting from scratch, there are tons of great free resources to get you started.

If you don't have brand colors and guidelines, use a free online color picker to choose 3-4 colors from an inspiration photo, or use a free color scheme creator to choose a color palette.

Black, white, and neutrals will always be the most highly shareable, so don't put pressure on yourself to make a really colorful, intentional brand identity. Black text on a white background is a great place to start.

One way you can batch create a lot of content and consistently invite new members to your community is by creating templates. With a few simple branded elements and colors, you can create 3-4 templates to rotate through.

BATCHED

Before you start creating content, especially to build a community page versus a personal brand, you want to batch as much photo and video assets as possible.

Whether you use stock footage or shoot your own, gather your assets and save them in a digital folder where you can easily access them. If you're using stock footage, try to choose imagery in similar color schemes so your brand is cohesive and easily recognizeable.

On the next page you'll see examples of what batched, templatized content using stock footage may look like. You can see how using a template will allow you to easily create multiple pieces of content at once, allowing you to create more and grow faster.

TEMPLATE EXAMPLES

The templates below were created in a paid Canva account, using free stock video from Pexels.com. We used a simple google search to find the font used on the Twitter app, uploaded it to Canva, and made a reel template of a "tweet." The same effect could be used by tweeting a quote, screenshotting the tweet, and laying it over a video.

The template allows you to easily batch 30 days of content in advance. If twitter is part of your overall strategy, you can also schedule those same tweets to go live at the same time as the corresponding TikToks or Reels. Social media is always changing, so stay up-to-date on current trends while sticking to systems that allow you to plan in advance.

REEL TEMPLATES

STORY TEMPLATES

WRITING
A BIO

TELL PEOPLE WHO YOU ARE

No matter which platform you choose, the first thing people will look at when they find your community page is your bio. Sometimes the only thing people will look at when they find your community page is your bio. Don't let it be the only thing people look at.

Good news is there's a simply formula that, in my experience, works regardless of platform. You may need to shorten, lengthen, add emojis, or slighlty adjust this formula based on your platform of choice, but this template will get you 90% of the way there.

If you're wondering how to make it the last 10%, study bios of top creators and pages on that platform. You'll start to see patterns, mirror that. Then, A/B test different options to see what works best. We'll talk more about A/B testing in phase three: adaptation. Don't get too hung up on making your bio perfect from day one, just get started.

BIO FORMULA

EXPLANATION: Making a good first impression applies the same in the digital world as it does in the physical one. Think of your bio, profile picture, and username like a handshake, eye contact, and introduction. You want to convey confidence and clarity. A good formula or rule of thumb for a social media bio generally looks like this:

OUTLINE	PROMPT
Who You Are	What category does this page fit into? A good format for this for a personal brand might be serious thing 1, serious thing 2, and silly thing 3. For a community page this may be a tagline or mission statement.
What You Do	More specifically, what can you do for them? What do you help people to know, feel, or accomplish?
Social Proof	What proof can you provide that this is a credible community with reputable referrals? This may be news features, or even something as simple as including the location or the name of the founder to show a real person is behind the community.
CTA	A strong call-to-action letting people know what steps to take next to learn more, go deeper, or build stronger connections to the community. This may be a free resource, a link to a podcast, or a coming soon page.

BIO TEMPLATE

Use this space to brainstorm your bio. For each section, brainstorm 2-3 options, then circle your favorite. Congrats! You've just crafted a clear, concise bio and an open invitation to your new community.

WHO	
WHAT	
PROOF	
CTA	

PROFILE PICTURES

There are two types of profile photos: the headshot and the logo. For either option, you want to be sure to use clear, high quality images, contrasting colors, and proper cropping. Take a minute to choose your profile photo and properly format it. Then, save it to your community google drive for

HEADSHOTS			
	POOR	BETTER	BEST
	Blurry, poor quality and cropping	High quality image, but too far away	High quality, intimate tight shot

BRAND LOGOS			
	GOODTYPE	GOODTYPE	
	POOR	BETTER	BEST
	White background	Too small to read in most places	Strong contrast, clear branding

PHASE TWO

ADOPTION

01 INVITATION

02 ADOPTION

03 ADAPTION

04 EXPANSION

CONTENT CATEGORIES

There are a few core archetypes of social media content. Of course, there are exceptions, but most content people consume online falls into one of these categories.

Typically, a powerful community page will consistently post two types of content, for example, educational and inspirational. This helps community members know exactly what to expect from your community page.

The more types of content you post, the more confusing it is for followers and the less likely they are to know how to engage with you. Choose 1-2 content types that makes the most sense for your brand.

If you're not sure where to start, look at a few similar communities or social media pages you like and want to emulate. What kind of content do they share?

For example, if you're running for political office, one of your core content categories should likely be sharing news. This can be images of articles with more commentary, video clips from news segments, or quotes from experts on a topic.

NEWS

Trending, story-driven content with the intent to inform an audience on current events, news, research, and worldviews

Goal social interaction: Saves, comments, shares

"That's interesting"

Pros:
There is always a fresh cycle of news, and endless content topics to choose from. Plus, it's generally a highly engaged topic and something people want to share their commentary or two cents on (read: engagement).

Cons:
Often controversial and divisive content. Use intentionally to attract and repel people to your core values and mission.

If you have a skincare company, maybe you share primarily educational content about your products. This can be infographics, images with text over it, or short entertaining videos that teach people about a specific topic or product.

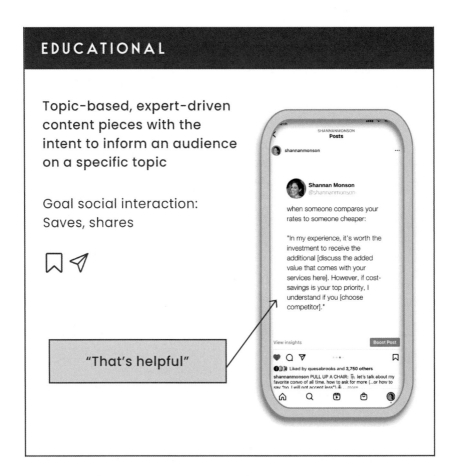

Pros:
Our brains are wired for curiosity, so people love to consume content that makes them smarter. It's also highly shareable because it's an easy way we can add value to someone else without creating the content ourselves.

Cons:
Can be overwhelming or hard to follow. Stick to simple, digestible content in highly visual formats.

Entertaining content is typically a core category for personal brands and comedians. It can also be a great secondary category to add humor, joy, and lighten topics that can be dry or otherwise boring.

ENTERTAINING

Funny or humorous content with the intent of making people laugh, smile, or be generally entertained

Goal social interaction:

"That's hilarious"

Pros:
Entertaining content is probably the most shareable content category, making it extremely valuable for growth. Plus, we build stronger bonds with people and communities who make us smile, laugh, and feel joy.

Cons:
It can be difficult to create original content in this category. Don't be afraid to re-post (with credit and permission).

This is one of the most widely used categories in digital communities because it inspires people to take action. It's easy to consume, makes us feel good about ourselves, and motivates people to create positive change.

INSPIRATIONAL

Motivational, thought leadership content pieces meant to inspire people to take action, feel better, or feel empowered in their life

Goal social interaction: Saves, comments, shares

"That's inspiring"

if you need a little inspiration to go after everything they said you couldn't, read this
@shannanmonson

Liked by yenniper and 2,490 others
shannanmonson just a little INSPIRATION to go after that thing. it's never too late.
... more
View all 92 comments
ashleyhcribb Legit starting to say 'just what the doctor ordered' from here.on.out.
February 1

Pros:
As humans our brains are wired to maximize pleasure, and this kind of content makes people feel good. It's easy to consume, easy to share, and fairly easy to create.

Cons:
Without context it can feel a bit "fluffy." Be sure to add context (like educational content) to establish your brand.

CONTENT STRATEGY

What categories of content fit your community best?

_____

_____

Choose a primary category and a secondary category.

1. _____

2. _____

How will these types of posts compliment your mission?

_____

_____

_____

Find three examples of content in each of your chosen categories. What do you like about each example? What learnings will you implement?

1. _____

_____

_____

2. _____

_____

_____

3. _____

_____

_____

CONTENT FORMATS

Whether it's a YouTube video, a podcast, or a 15-second TikTok...ultimately, all content follows the same (or at least very similar) formula. It starts with a hook, moves into the value of the content piece, and then finishes with a call to action. If you can find evidence against this, I'd be excited to see it. But in my experience, every piece of content follows this same formula.

What's really exciting about this is it means you don't have to reinvent the wheel. The format in which we share content is constantly evolving, but the core message is not. (Read that again.) Ten years ago a long-format blog post was the gold standard, then podcasts, and now, short-form video. The message, however, stays the same.

Sometimes new content creators or community builders feel overwhelmed by how quickly the internet changes. It can feel exhausting trying to keep up with new algorithms, new and emerging platforms, and constantly changing trends. But if you realize all you need to do is slightly adapt what you're already doing, suddenly it becomes much more manageable.

Another interesting thing happens with new emerging trends and platforms, early adopters get rewarded. If you're willing to stay open-minded and try new things, you'll always be ahead of the curve.

MACRO VS. MICRO

Think of content in two groups:

(1) macro content: longer format content like podcast episodes, YouTube videos, and blog posts, and
(2) micro content: shorter format content like TikToks, Reels, Instagram posts, Linked In posts, etc.

There's no rule of thumb because content is changing so quickly. For some content strategies macro content might be an hour long podcast, for others it might be a 1 minute video. The goal is creating more comprehensive pieces of content that you can pull micro derivatives from.

For example, if you have an hour long podcast, maybe you edit a 1 minute video for an Instagram reel, use three direct quotes as both tweets and Instagram static posts, and a shortened version of the transcript as a carousel post.

This will look different for every strategy, but it should be streamlined and intentional so that you can quickly and easily create your macro content, and then break it into multiple additional pieces of micro content.

MACRO

5-minute video interview on how to ask for more money

MICRO

10 tweets with scripts for different scenarios

CONTENT TEMPLATES

Content creation clicked when I realized...it's just a formula. Just like movies follow storytelling formulas, content does too. After all, at the end of the day it's all just storytelling.

Once you realize this, rather than starting from scratch, you can start from experience. (The best place to start, in my opinion.) On the next few pages you'll find some of my favorite tried-and-tested formulas. These are concepts I've used hundreds of times in hundreds of different ways with incredible success, and the baseline for 90% of my content creation process.

When you're creating content, it can be tempting to whip out your phone and record a video, to start writing a caption, or to simply take a photo and hit post. You can do this, absolutely, but especially if your goal is scalable growth, starting with a system will 10x your results.

Systems and workflows allow you to batch create content which is absolutely vital as your community grows and more people are involved in the content creation process. To the right you'll find an overview of the content creation process and what this can look like for you. As your community grows, each step of this process will become the responsibility of a different team member.

On the next few pages you'll find templates to guide you through step two: the writing process.

CONTENT CREATION PROCESS

STEP ONE: RESEARCH

Start with a topic or idea

Use SEO research, research from top accounts in your niche, and viral content research to brainstorm.

STEP TWO: WRITE

Write the copy

Use a template or formula to write the copy for your content. Start with the hook and end with a CTA.

STEP FOUR: PRODUCE

Produce the content

Record, design, edit... produce the content based off the format you chose and get it ready to publish.

STEP THREE: FORMAT

Decide the format

What format tells the story best? Will it be a video? Podcast? Carousel? Photo and caption? Make a plan.

STEP FIVE: REVIEW

Review the content

Check for errors, make sure the content is in line with community values and brand guidelines, and schedule it to post.

STEP SIX: PUBLISH

Publish the content

Congrats! It's time to put your content out into the world and engage with your community.

MISSION

EXPLANATION: The mission post is your stake in the ground signifying where your community stands, what you set out to accomplish, and how potential new members can be involved. The goal is to elicit a strong emotional response and define the purpose of the community. This post should be easily accessible as a pinned post or highlight.

OUTLINE	PROMPT
Current State	Shocking or surprising statistic that portrays the problem your community was built to solve.
Belief	A futuristic belief statement arguing that a better reality is possible.
Call to Arms	Activate your audience by inviting them to support the mission and create a better future.
Action Step	Let them know where to begin, what step to take next, or how you want them to be involved.
Hopeful Message	Leave them with a message of hope for the better world you will build together.
Gratitude	Express gratitude for joining the community and being part of the change.

WHEN TO USE: As an introduction post to welcome new members, or after an influx of new growth and members.

CONTENT COPY

Use this space to outline the copy for your content. Once you decide the core content, you can determine the best format, whether it's voice over for a video, graphics for a carousel, or in text in a caption.

HOOK	
INTRO	
PART I	
PART II	
PART III	
CTA	

HOW IT WORKS

EXPLANATION: The goal is to let the viewer know (1) who you are, (2) why your community exists, and (3) what they can expect to gain by being a part of it. This post should be evergreen, easy to find, and readily accessible by interested new members. Think: pinned to the top of your community page or saved as a highlight.

OUTLINE	PROMPT
Problem	Identify the problem your community exists to solve. "Did you know…"
Vision	"What if there was a way it could (paint the vision your mission statement aims to accomplish)."
Mission Statement	Put your stake in the ground and let people rally around it. "That's exactly what we set out to do…"
Process	Explain how you plan to accomplish the mission. "First, we are…"
Invitation	Invite them to be a part of the solution. "Join us and let's do this together."
Call-to-Action	Invite them to join the community and take action towards the mission, too.

WHEN TO USE: To tell your founder story or explain how your product or service works.

CONTENT COPY

Use this space to outline the copy for your content. Once you decide the core content, you can determine the best format, whether it's voice over for a video, graphics for a carousel, or in text in a caption.

INTRO HOOK	
PART I	
PART II	
PART III	
CTA	

TRANSFORMATION

EXPLANATION: The transformation post is an inspirational story meant to position the storyteller as the empathetic guide or expert who has struggled with the problem before, felt the same pain points, and found a better way. The post should inspire the viewer to take action to begin the transformation, too.

OUTLINE	PROMPT
Problem	If you're struggling with this problem, this is for you.
Old World	Before, the situation was (describe the old world)…And what was frustrating about this was (describe the pain points)…
Inciting Incident	And then one day, something happened (describe the inciting incident)…
New World	Today, this is my new reality (describe the new, better world)…
Process	Here's what I did to get here (describe the transformation process)…
Invitation	Invite them to take the journey, too.
CTA	Call to action to take the next step.

WHEN TO USE: As a regular content piece to show your community impact and to spotlight case studies.

CONTENT COPY

Use this space to outline the copy for your content. Once you decide the core content, you can determine the best format, whether it's voice over for a video, graphics for a carousel, or in text in a caption.

HOOK	
INTRO	
PART I	
PART II	
PART III	
CTA	

EDUCATION

EXPLANATION: The education post is an in-depth training on a core pillar or foundational concept relevant to your community. The goal is to provide product or process information that provides the viewer with tools and resources to take the next step in the journey. This should be easily digestible, actionable, and mission-driven.

OUTLINE	PROMPT
Problem	Identify the specific problem relevant to this particular pillar or concept.
Pain	Define the pain living with this problem causes, and empathize with the pain. points.
Introduction	Introduce a learning lesson or topic that will address or help solve this problem.
Process	Break down the step-by-step teaching points, resources, or knowledge the viewer needs to learn.
Cement	Cement the validity of this training with evidance (testimonials, statistics, or social proof).
Call-to-Action	Invite them to share with other people and invite them to join the community.

WHEN TO USE: As a regular content piece to educate your community and inspire them to take action.

CONTENT COPY

Use this space to outline the copy for your content. Once you decide the core content, you can determine the best format, whether it's voice over for a video, graphics for a carousel, or in text in a caption.

HOOK	INTRO	PART I	PART II	PART III	CTA

TESTIMONIAL

EXPLANATION: The testimonial post is a quote, video, or review post that provides social proof that the process or product works. The goal is to show the viewer that if they adapt this new set of ideas, they will have a positive outcome, too. These testimonials provide overwhelming evidence to support the new ideas presented.

OUTLINE	PROMPT
Hook	A shocking or enticing opening line to pull the viewer in. "I never thought this would happen."
Result	Describe the dream scenario. "Right now, I'm living the dream...(which looks like)"
Meaning	Apply meaning. "What this means is I'm now...(describe the pleasure that comes from this result)
Advice	Provide a nudge for someone still living with the problem. "If I could go back in time I'd tell myself..."
Review	Recommend or give a review for the product or process. "I can't recommend this enough..."
CTA	Invite them to take the journey, too.

WHEN TO USE: As a regular content piece to inspire, motivate, and create positive change within your community.

CONTENT COPY

Use this space to outline the copy for your content. Once you decide the core content, you can determine the best format, whether it's voice over for a video, graphics for a carousel, or in text in a caption.

INTRO HOOK	PART I	PART II	PART III	CTA	

CONVERSATION

EXPLANATION: The conversation post is something that starts a conversation. It may be a surface-level, brief reaction or it may be an in-depth, conversational debate. Either way, the goal is to elicit an emotional response, give the viewer something to think about, and encourage them to engage in the conversation.

OUTLINE	PROMPT
Question	Ask a question. Examples include yes/no, would you rather, or which resonates most 1-3.
Debate	Objectively share one side of the argument, as well as a glimpse into the other.
Re-Post	Share community responses alongside your own commentary, thoughts, or follow up questions.
Ask	Ask the community again, after reviewing the arguments, what conclusion they've come to.
Activate	Encourage the community to take action. They've reached a conclusion, now what?
Gratitude	Express gratitude to your community for participating in the conversation.

WHEN TO USE: As a regular content piece to start conversations and curate engagement and connection.

CONTENT COPY

Use this space to outline the copy for your content. Once you decide the core content, you can determine the best format, whether it's voice over for a video, graphics for a carousel, or in text in a caption.

INTRO HOOK		
PART I		
PART II		
PART III		
CTA		

VISION CASTING

EXPLANATION: The inspiration post is a vision-casting exercise meant to inspire hope, activate behavior change, and set in motion positive change. The goal is to leave the viewer feeling hopeful, to overcome potential obstacles, and give the viewer a deeper belief in themself. It helps the viewer visualize a better future than they have right now.

OUTLINE	PROMPT
Vision	Picture this...(describe the dream scenario)
Meaning	Apply meaning. "What would it mean to you/feel like to... (experience the dream scenario)"
Proof	Provide proof this future is possible either with parallel situations, statistics, etc.
Blockers	Identify the obstacles or barriers to change. What's preventing this new future.
Tools	Give the viewer tools to break through the blockers, and remove the current obstacles.
Invitation	Invite the viewer to use the tools to help the community bring the vision to life.

WHEN TO USE: Before launching a new initiative or product, to hype community members about what's possible.

CONTENT COPY

Use this space to outline the copy for your content. Once you decide the core content, you can determine the best format, whether it's voice over for a video, graphics for a carousel, or in text in a caption.

HOOK	INTRO	PART I	PART II	PART III	CTA

COUNTEROBJECTION

EXPLANATION: The counterobjection post is an opportunity to respond to push back, whether it's from your own community members of opposing viewpoints. The goal is to help the viewer see an alternative perspective. This strategy helps to attract your ideal community members and repel others.

OUTLINE	PROMPT
Objection	State the objection.
Acknowledge	Acknowledge where the objection is coming from, whether it's a person, viewpoint, or perspective.
Counter	Provide a counter-objection.
Proof	Backup your counter-objection with proof, statistics, or research to meet your claim.
CTA	Invite the viewer to share if they agree or take action to support the mission.

WHEN TO USE: After launching a new initiative or product, to remove barriers to action and motivate change.

CONTENT COPY

Use this space to outline the copy for your content. Once you decide the core content, you can determine the best format, whether it's voice over for a video, graphics for a carousel, or in text in a caption.

HOOK	
INTRO	
PART I	
PART II	
PART III	
CTA	

STARTING CONVERSATIONS

IT'S A MARATHON, NOT A SPRINT.

Community building is a marathon, not a sprint. People are people, whether you connect with them online or in person. It might not seem intuitive at first on the internet, but your number one goal should always be connection. If someone sends a message asking you a question, take the time to build a connection before you answer. Say hello. Tell them how happy you are to connect with them. Take 15 seconds to scroll through their profile and find a common ground to connect over. Give them a genuine compliment.

If someone asked you, "what's the price?" or "do you have these in yellow?" in real life you wouldn't say yes and then just stop talking. You'd greet them. Compliment their style choices, ask about what they're shopping for, you'd be a human. Be a human online, too. (Or tell your social media managers and virtual assistants to be humans, too.)

Your goal should always be to open the loop, rather than close it, and keep the conversation going as long as possible. Yes, as long as possible. We're building community, not checking boxes. For example, a closed loop response to the question, "do you have these in yellow?" might look like, "yes, we do." Silence. The end. The loop is closed. Instead, find ways to open a new loop. That might look like, "Yes, we do! What are you shopping for? I'd love to hear more about what you're looking for." Create opportunities to continue the conversation. Go deeper. Build the relationship, don't just finish the transaction.

CREATE MICRO MOMENTS

Think about the humans you have the deepest connections with. They likely either make you laugh, listen to your pain and frustrations, or inspire you to be a better human. Right? Think of your online interactions, comments, and direct messages, in the same way. Is there an opportunity to make this person laugh? Can you send a voice message and connect in a more meaningful way? Can you send a meme or quote that inspires?

Stop thinking of comments like a checklist you need to complete and start thinking of them as an experience you get the opportunity to create. Your goal isn't to respond, your goal is to elicit a strong emotion. A deep belly laugh. A full body hug. A soul-piercing moment of realization. Or, you can just respond, "yes." Totally up to you.

One of the most interesting phenomena I've experienced in the past decade of building digital communities is just how long it takes someone to go from casual viewer, to follower, to community member, and eventually, loyal brand ambassador. The biggest disservice you can do for yourself (or your company, organization, or mission) is to prioritize today's transaction over next year's raving fan. Trust the process, and train for the marathon.

Yes, it's slow. Yes, it's time consuming responding to hundreds (sometimes thousands) of comments and messages. But you are filling a relational bucket. Every comment, every DM, every heart, is a drop in the bucket. It might feel like it's not worth it right now, but if you keep at it, in a year you'll have enough to fill a small ocean. If you only take one piece of advice from this workbook, let it be this: Never underestimate the power of filling your relationship bucket.

CALLS TO ACTION

One of the most important aspects of building community is cultivating connections between members. Content can feel like a one-sided conversation, but it shouldn't be. Remember you are hosting space for people to talk, not talking at people. Here are some common call-to-actions that work well to start conversations. Remember to personalize these, adapt to the voice and tone of your community, and test to see what works best for your brand.

- Which one resonate most 1-10 and why?
- Tag a friend who needs to hear this.
- Share this with someone you love.
- Can you relate? Tell me about a time you...
- Leave an below if you agree.
- Tag 3 people who...
- Save this post for...
- Comment "Yes" if you...
- What are your thoughts on...
- Send this to a friend who ....
- Share your thoughts in the comments.

ENGAGEMENT CHECKLIST:

☐ Is it easy to engage in a few words or emojis?

☐ Is it comfortable to engage publicly? Do I mind if friends or family see?

☐ Is it interesting to engage? Is this a conversation I care to join?

CREATING EXPERIENCES
TO SURPISE AND DELIGHT

Your goal, in building a strong community, is to connect people to powerful feelings. Every single touch point you have with your community, whether it's a social media post, a website page, or a text message, should create an experience.

One way to create experiences is to invoke emotions. Think of all the witty sayings you see on the side of buildings that make you feel a certain way. They make you laugh, make you feel empowered, make you cry...they're short, micro messages that create an experience.

Start paying attention to moments, out in the wild or online, that make you feel a certain way. What are they? How did they make you feel? Start with the emotion you want to evoke (laughter, joy, inspiration, etc) and work backwards.

One of the most powerful emotions you can invoke is the element of surprise. Think of the last time you were surprised with a gift, or got a dessert for free at a restaurant. What feeling did that invoke? Likely a positive one. You likely felt a positive emotional connection.

Start to think of places you can surprise and delight people. Maybe it's in your content with a surprising plot twist at the end. Maybe it's by sending a personalized voice memo welcoming someone to the community. Maybe it's a free gift...look for opportunities to create experiences that invoke emotions at every touch point in your community.

YOU'LL NEVER KNOW UNLESS YOU TRY IS REALLY UNDERUTILIZED ADVICE. YOU'LL NEVER KNOW UNLESS YOU TRY IT AGAIN DIFFERENTLY. YOU'LL NEVER KNOW UNLESS YOU'RE WILLING TO START OVER AS MANY TIMES AS IT TAKES TO GET IT RIGHT.

PHASE THREE

ADAPTION

01 INVITATION

02 ADOPTION

03 ADAPTION

04 EXPANSION

ADAPTING WITH ANALYTICS

The best thing you can do at this stage of community building is create as much content as possible. Test everything. Compare every piece of content you put out. If you're only putting out 1-2 pieces of content a week, it's going to take a lot of time to learn and understand what works best. On the flip side, if you put out 1-2 pieces of content a day, you're going to learn really quickly what works and what doesn't.

Don't worry about putting out too much content, chances are it's not going to get pushed to that many people to begin with. Your goal is quantity, especially at the beginning, and as you learn more you can adapt and put out more hyper-target quality content.

There's three metrics I suggest prioritizing above other data: (1) shares, how many people are organically sharing your content, (2) follows, how many people are hitting follow after consuming your content, and (3) reach, how many people is your content reaching in the first place. If you can increase these three numbers, your community grows. It's that simple.

There are different softwares you can use to analyze data, and depending on which platform you are prioritizing, pros and cons to each. For the purposes of this example, we'll look at analytics inside the Instagram insights, filtered by shares, follows, and reach.

First, look for common themes. Are there topics that consistently get more shares? More follows? More reach For example, you'll see common themes in the top shared posts on my personal brand account: rest, saying no, and asking for more money.

You'll also see a lot of overlap, topics that reach more people, get more follows. That logically makes sense. So what I recommend you look for are posts that get a lot of reach or shares but *don't* turn into follows. Sometimes things are highly shareable, but don't really relate back to your mission or the purpose of your community.

For example, the post "7 of the most encouraging things to say to a friend" was widely shared and reached a lot of people. That makes sense, it's encouraging, uplifting, and a nice change of pace from some of my regular content about saying no and standing up for yourself. It's good content, but it didn't grow the community because it's not really related to the mission. How do I know this?

Because I've extensively tested thousands of topics and can tell you with 80% (ish) accuracy what content works and what doesn't. That's the kind of feedback you can only get with data.

Study your content every single week, repeat the same topic in a different format, test, A/B test, and test again. This is an ongoing process. The more you review your analytics and adopt accordingly, the more your community will grow.

RESPONDING
WITH CONTENT

LEADING CONVERSATIONS

Your role as community curator is simply to host and lead a conversation, not to dominate it. The best thing you can do to build true community is give your members a voice. The most basic way to do this is to repond to comments, answer questions, and re-post community members content, like this. This also looks like duets, stitches, and reaction videos to other people's content.

Maybe it's question boxes in stories, or using a question or comment to make a new piece of content. The point is this content is made *in a direct response* to something your community said. Meaning, it's your job as the leader to be listening. You don't need thousands of people to do this either. Respond to the one person who is engaging and that 1 person will turn into one hundred.

The next level of responsive content is leveraging user-generated content (UGC) to create even better content.

For example, I shared that my son was doing a Shark Tank competition at school, and said, "wouldn't it be fun if we did our own?" The response was overwhelmingly, "yes."

I created simple requirements to participate, and asked members to post their submission in their Instagram stories and tag me. Hundreds of community members posted about it on their own stories and posted submissions.

Then, thousands of people tuned in to watch the reposts on my stories, casting their votes for the winner. This is a great example of responsive content and UGC. I didn't create the content, I simply led it and held space for the community. Brainstorm ways you can do this in your own community.

A/B TESTING
IF IT'S WORKING WORK IT HARDER

The absolute best thing you can do when you're working with analytics is to focus on optimizing what's already working. Did you have a post that reached a new audience, brought in new members, or connected deeply with your current members? Congrats! Your goal should be to do the same thing again, three different ways.

Maybe you try the exact same content re-purposed into a different format (i.e. from a carousel to a video). Maybe you take the same video and change out the hook (the first 5 seconds) and compare the results. Don't be afraid to post the same thing twice, the same thing with a slightly different adaptation, or the same thing in a different format.

This is how you learn what topics your audience wants to talk about, what formats they want to consume content, and the best voice for your message and mission. Here's a great way to get started with A/B testing. Search your top performing content in the past year. Take your top 5 best posts, and re-format each one to post again. Then, compare and contrast the data. What worked well? What didn't? How can we use this data to build better?

Once you get into a good flow, I recommend re-purposing your best content at least once a month, maybe more depending on how often you post. Remember, you might have been saying the same thing for years, but your new community members, and the people who have just found you, haven't heard it yet, haven't heard in in this way, or they need to hear it again in order to take action towards the mission.

PHASE FOUR

EXPANSION

01 INVITATION

02 ADOPTION

03 ADAPTION

04 EXPANSION

THE ART & SCIENCE OF
VIRAL POSTS

WHAT IS A VIRAL POST?

A viral post is something that is (1) highly shareable and (2) reaches a significantly large audience than your average organic reach. You can typically identify a viral post because it has 5x or more the numbers of likes, comments, or views as an average post on that particular community page. Virality is a formula, and it's more science than art. Let's look at the anatomy of a viral post.

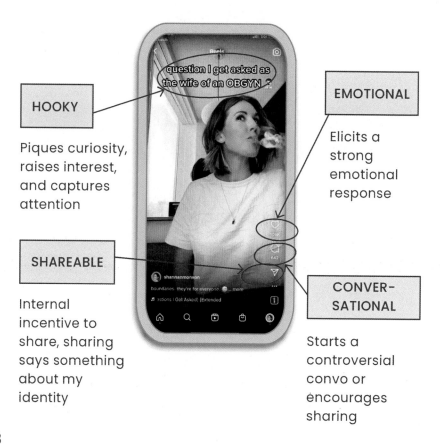

HOOKY

Piques curiosity, raises interest, and captures attention

EMOTIONAL

Elicits a strong emotional response

SHAREABLE

Internal incentive to share, sharing says something about my identity

CONVER-SATIONAL

Starts a controversial convo or encourages sharing

ANATOMY OF VIRALITY

Viral content typically contains at least 4 of 5 of the following elements. This is the "science" of virality-that combined with art and luck-makes up a viral post.

☐ **HOOKY** Raises at least one other question	What I wish someone told me... Watch this if you want to... 3 things you didn't know about...
☐ **EMOTIONAL** Elicits a strong and immediate emotional reaction	Sentimental "aww" Anger "absolutely not" Pride "this is me!" Joy "this is so pure" Happiness "laughing so hard"
☐ **CONVERSATIONAL** Easy to add to the conversation	Controversial: Strongly Agree/Disagree Experience Shares: "This happened to me, too"
☐ **SHAREABLE** Says something about your identity	Shares knowledge that reflects positively on you as the sharer Spreads joy, laughter or education that makes people perceive you as smart, etc
☐ **SURPRISING** Has a plot twist you didn't see coming	There's an element of surprise that, in and of itself, delights us. The surprise heightens the emotion.

PSYCHOLOGY OF SHARING

WHY PEOPLE SHARE

As a general rule, things that are highly shareable appeal to a person's core identity. By sharing this piece of content online, they are:

Making a statement about who they are, how they see themselves as a person, and what they stand for

Making a statement about who they want other people to think they are, how they want to be perceived by others

Making a statement about who they want to become, their highest self, who they want to be in the future

Here's a few examples of quotes that are highly shareable, and how they speak to a person's core identity.

WHAT I SHARE:	WHAT IT SAYS ABOUT ME:
Due to personal reasons, I will not be explaining myself to anyone anymore. →	I am the kind of person who sets boundaries and doesn't waste time with trivial things.
Invoice: cutting one wire $1, knowing which wire to cute $999, total: $1000 →	I am an expert and my skills are valuable. I shouldn't need to justify my rates.
You are moving forward and sometimes moving forward means taking two steps back. →	I may not be achieving the things I said I would, but I'm not failing, I'm just moving at my own pace.

HOW TO GO VIRAL

There are really only two options to go viral. Either you (1) re-post someone else's viral content-with proper credit, permission, and attribution-or (2) you create your own viral content. The latter is the ideal scenario because you own the content, have full control over how it looks, the goals it accomplishes, etc.

However, virality isn't all science. It's also an art form and a bit of luck. You may create 100 pieces of phenomenal content with viral components…and only have 1 piece go viral. Which is why the most proven way to grow your community is leveraging already proven viral content.

OVERNIGHT SUCCESS IS A LIE. ONE HIT WONDERS ARE RARE. DON'T TRY TO BE THE EXCEPTION, BE THE RULE. BE THE PERSON WHO WAS A SLOW, BORING BURN. THAT'S HOW YOU WIN.

HOW TO SOURCE VIRAL CONTENT

1. TWITTER ADVANCED SEARCH

Because twitter is primarily a text-first platform, it has the capability to search keywords, phrases, and rank data easily for you. You can search keywords and phrases related to your mission, your core community values, or even educational topics you are creating content around. Use this functionality to find ideas and concepts that have gone viral, reaching a significantly larger audience than the original creator's. Be sure to ask for permission and provide proper credit if you re-post a tweet or quote.

2. COMMUNITY PAGES

Another way to find viral content within your niche or industry is to search already established pages. There are many social media pages that are exclusively re-posts of other people's content. Often, these pages are easy to find with specific hashtag research and are only re-posts of top viral content. You can also go to top creator's pages and find their best of the best content. The posts with exponentially more likes, comments, and views than average.

3. EXPLORE PAGES

Social media apps want you to spend more time exploring content on their app, so the "Explore" or "For You" pages will show you more content similar to what you've already engaged with. By intentionally engaging with niche specific content, you can train your algorithm to show you the best of the best in that category.

TWITTER ADVANCED SEARCH

KEYWORD

Go to twitter.com/search-advanced. You can search by viral trends like "I don't know who needs to hear this but..." or "due to personal reasons," by topic such as "hustle culture" "4 day work week," or core values such as "rest" "boundaries" or "diversity." Search by shareability by adding a filter for "minimum retweets" or by engagement by adding a filter for "minimum replies." 10,000 plus is a good place to start for sourcing viral content.

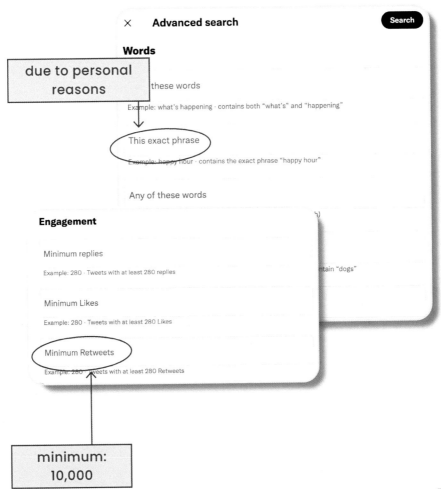

COMMUNITY PAGE RESEARCH

STUDYING MEANINGFUL SOCIAL INTERACTIONS

One of the best ways to find top performing content is to find thought leaders in your niche or large community pages, and then analyze their content. What are the average statistics of their meaningful social interactions (likes, comments, views)? Which posts receive significantly higher than that average? Those are the posts you want to re-post, to study, and to learn from. The same goes for smaller pages and creators. If their average video view is 1k, and you see a post that got 7k, pay attention to why that video worked. What's different about it? What are the central themes? Use this strategy to both learn how to make better content and to find content to re-post to build your community.

CAPTURING ATTENTION

THE NUMBER ONE RULE OF STORYTELLING:

If it doesn't stop the scroll nothing else matters. The very first thing people see, the first 1-3 seconds of your video, podcast, or written content, either: (1) draws your audience in and convinces them to keep going or (2) doesn't grab their attention and they continue their scroll.

If someone doesn't take the time to stop scrolling on their feed and actually watch the rest of the video, listen to the rest of the podcast, or read the caption...it doesn't matter how phenomenal your content is, because no one will see it. The goal of a hook is to create an open loop. You want your hook to make people ask 10 more questions, you want them to stick around to see how it ends.

CREATE AN OPEN LOOP

A closed loop might look like: "Sh*t is a swear word." This is a fact. The point was made, we have no questions, no real desire for a debate, and the loop is closed. But on the other hand, "Why do you curse in front of your kids?" is an open loop. We want to know, what's the answer? What's your justification? Do we agree? Do we disagree? This is an example of a phenomenal hook for a parenting video. It's controversial, it's interesting, and regardless of which side of the debate we fall on, we want to enter the conversation (read: engagement).

HOOK FORMULAS

Viral content typically contains at least 4 of 5 of the following elements. This is the "science" of virality-that combined with art and luck-makes up a viral post.

☐ **TELL AN INTERESTING FACT** Did you know you used to be able to send babies through the mail?	Wait...what? This is shocking, surprising, and brings up more questions. When was this? How was this legal? Did anyone do it? This is a great hook because it opens a loop. Bonus points: it gives the viewer a fun conversation starter for their next dinner party. (Win win.)
☐ **START IN THE MIDDLE** "No, you don't work 9 to 5."	Use dialogue to start in the middle of a conversation or story. What's the setting? Who's talking? What did I miss? If it's a conversation that piques their interest, it makes the viewer want to join the conversation.
☐ **HOW TO SOLVE A PROBLEM** How to ask your boss for a raise	If the viewer is struggling with this particular problem, they're going to want to hear the advice. It raises questions like, "Is it good advice? Is it something I'm doing wrong? Is it something I want to try?"

HOOK IDEAS

Hooks are everywhere. Once you start to see the formulas, you won't be able to un-see them. Which is good, because remember: the only thing that matters to get people to finish the story is the hook. As content gets faster and attention spans get shorter, you'll notice a lot of hooks are visual hooks only. For example, as text on the screen but never spoken outloud, or an attention-grabbing visual instead of a written hook. The important thing is: attention.

- You're not going to believe this...
- The story of how I...
- What I wish someone had told me about...
- 7 myths about...
- Watch this if you want to...
- 3 things you didn't know about...
- Don't start your day without...
- You'll never believe what just happened...
- Want to see behind-the-scenes of...
- This might sound weird but...
- Don't make this mistake...
- Have you ever wondered...
- Confessions of a...
- 3 surprising ways to...
- What no one will tell you about...
- Don't do this thing without...

HOOK CHECKLIST:

- ☐ Does it raise another question?
- ☐ Does it invoke a strong emotion?
- ☐ Is it easy to understand?
- ☐ Does it grab attention?
- ☐ Does it encourage engagement?
- ☐ Can you read it in 5 seconds or less?

HOOK RESEARCH

Start looking for hooks in the wild. Write down your favorites. Keep a notes app of the best hooks you've seen. What do you like about each one? How can you use it as inspiration for your next story? A hook is the beginning of every great story ever told. Want to tell great stories? Start by creating great hooks.

_____

_____

_____

_____

_____

_____

_____

_____

_____

_____

_____

_____

_____

_____

CREATING
SOCIAL SYSTEMS

Now that you have a process for creating social content, the best thing you can do is create systems to batch your content. Take each step of the process, and turn it into a daily, weekly. monthly, or quarterly task.

For example, I recommend doing research on your macro content topics using SEO and other community pages once a quarter. Map out the topics your content will cover for the next three months. You'll also want to do viral content research every week. Trends change quickly, and this will allow you to get ahead with your content on a quarterly basis, while still staying relevant.

Your workflow will look different depending on how many team resources you have, how far in advance you want to plan, etc, but here's an example of what your social systems could look like.

Use a project management software to create a kanban board (to do, doing, done) to organize your workflow. My board looks like this from left to right: to write, to record, to produce, to approve, and to post.

I might have an idea about a salary negotiation post, so I'll create a task and move it to the "to write" column. Then when I sit down to write, I'll write 2-3 content pieces from that column and move then to the "to record" column, and so on. This allows you to always be working on multiple pieces of content at a time and to be the most efficient in your workflows instead of task hopping from writing, to editing, to producing, and so on.

SOCIAL SYSTEMS

QUARTERLY

Define goals

Review last quarter's growth, this quarter's goal, and do research to map out topics you'll cover the next 3 months.

MONTHLY

Research

Use SEO research and viral content research to create a framework for that month's posts. Write your titles, outlines, and schedule post dates.

WEEKLY

Write and Produce

Write the copy for each piece of content and produce it for publication. Schedule the post, caption, time, and hashtags.

DAILY

Post and Engage

Post your prepared content and engage with your community. Review analytics and make a plan to re-purpose best-performing content.

NOTE
FROM THE AUTHOR

**EVERYTHING SHIFTS
WHEN YOU REALIZE
THE PEOPLE WHO
HAVE DONE IT
BEFORE YOU ARE NOT
SMARTER THAN YOU,
THEY JUST STARTED
AND DIDN'T STOP
UNTIL THEY FIGURED
IT OUT.**

CREATOR'S MINDSET

YOUR FIRST DRAFT IS GOING TO SUCK.

It's not the world's most encouraging first line, I know, but it's important. It's important because not only will it not be good, but there's a good chance no one will see it.

And sometimes that's the hardest part. Not getting recognition for your work. The amount of time that you will spend ideating, creating, editing, and posting content that nobody ever sees is something that I want you to get comfortable with right now.

Everyone starts out a beginner. Creating work that no one sees is a big part of the learning curve. You have to get comfortable writing when no one is reading, creating when no one is consuming, putting in the hours when you know no one is clapping, no one is listening, no one is watching. That's it. That's the big secret.

And I promise, if you can push through the crappy first drafts, if you're willing to suck long enough to become proficient, one day your work won't just be good enough, it will be excellent. It won't just be seen, it will be applauded. People will call you talented, but you and I will both know what deep down you've known all along, talent didn't get you here, hard work did.

READY TO

GO DEEPER?

Scan the QR code below to learn
more about implementing the
Community First framework.

ABOUT THE AUTHOR

Shannan Monson is a serial entrepreneur, viral storyteller, and community growth expert who's built multiple seven-figure businesses, supported hundreds of other business owners from zero to six and seven figures, and inspires hundreds of thousands of people every day via her highly-engaged social media platforms.

Shannan was one of the first people to truly learn to leverage social media for digital community-building, taking what initially started out as a side hustle in the early days of Instagram to a self-funded six-figure business, complete with a wellness studio and storefront marketed exclusively through social media.

She has since consulted for some of the fastest-growing lifestyle companies in the world, in industries ranging from wellness to entrepreneurship, and she is regularly featured on NBC, ABC, Entrepreneur, and Good Morning America.

Whether she's helping a venture-backed start-up reach their first 50K followers, or teaching entrepreneurs the techniques she uses to bootstrap businesses and reach over one million people per month, it all comes back to the same thing: her unshakeable belief in the power of owning your unique voice to make a bigger impact.

Follow Shannan on all social platforms @shannanmonson for more tips to be a better leader and community builder. For speaking or consulting inquiries, please contact hello@ shannanmonson.com.

RESOURCE

LIBRARY

INVITATION

ADOPTION

EXPANSION

Made in the USA
Columbia, SC
10 May 2023

16159269R00049